The Sunflower Journey

Plant The Seed and Watch It Grow!

SHELLY LAROQUE

Printed in the United States of America

First Printing, 2020

ISBN 978-0-5782-4241-5

Acknowledgements

To God be the glory for the idea and inspiration for this beautiful book. Special thanks to my husband for tending to the garden. My friend, Peyton Procaccini, thank you for all your help in assisting me with the editing of this work. Finally, many thanks to those who wish to remain anonymous whose work in formatting and layout allowed this work to come to fruition.

The sun is shining, the garden is ready,
how exciting this journey will be!

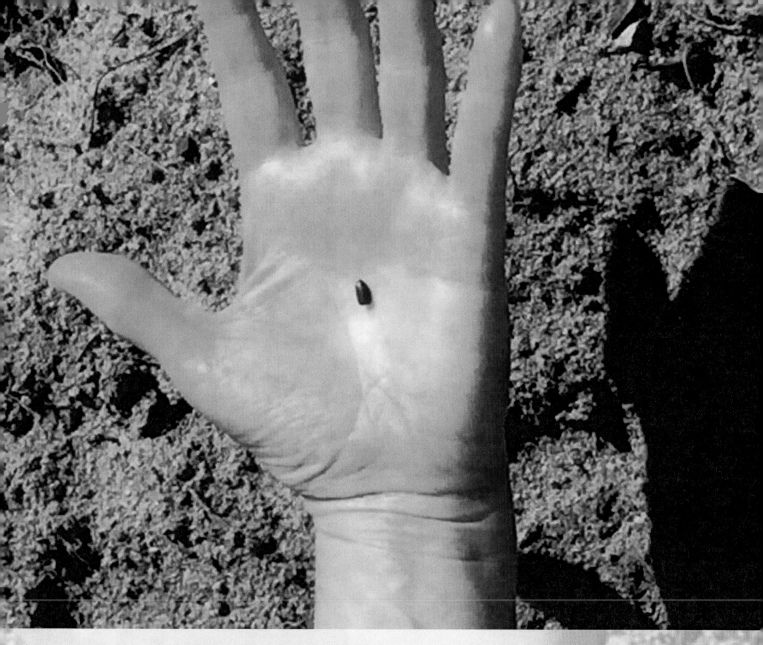

Now you're ready as the seed is in your hand.
Let's count 1, 2, 3, plant it in the ground and
watch it grow! Hold on, here we go!

Aww... Look! A baby sprout has broken through the ground.

"Forget the former things; do not dwell on the past. See, I am doing a new thing! Now it springs up; do you not perceive it? I am making a way in the wilderness and streams in the wasteland."
Isaiah 43:18-19

WOW, look at how tall the
sunflower plants are getting!

Oh look! The sunflower is starting to form, and we have a new lady bug friend!

Look, the sunflower is beginning to open and the middle looks like yarn!

"For you created my inmost being; you knit me together in my mother's womb. I praise you because I am fearfully and wonderfully made; your works are wonderful, I know that full well."
Psalm 139:13-14

The first three sunflowers have bloomed...
Notice how they all are beautifully different.

The morning dew makes
the sunflower shine.

*"Let my teaching fall like rain and my words
descend like dew, like showers on new grass,
like abundant rain on tender plants."*
Deuteronomy 32:2

Aww... the Momma sunflower is looking over her newborn baby.

"The Lord will watch over your coming and going both now and forevermore."
Psalm 121:8

How fun, let's play peek-a-boo!

*Jesus said, "Let the little children come to me,
and do not hinder them, for the kingdom of
heaven belongs to such as these."*
Matthew 19:14

Even though the sunflowers are very tall,
did you know Gods love is higher!

"For great is your love higher than the heavens;
your faithfulness reaches to the skies."
Psalm 108:4

Buzz, Buzz, Buzz, can you find all the bees around the sunflowers on both pages?

It's fun buzzing around planting seeds by sharing the love of Jesus!

"I planted the seed, Apollos watered it, but God has been making it grow."
1 Corinthians 3:6

"Therefore, encourage one another and build each other up, just as in fact you are doing."
1 Thessalonians 5:11

Do you see the yellow sunflower peeking in?

Then Jesus spoke to them again, saying, "I am the light of the world. He who follows Me shall not walk in darkness, but have the light of life." John 8:12 NKJV

When I looked at the middle sunflower I thought
of the crown of thorns, and the following Bible
verses and how much we are loved!

"For God so loved the world, that he gave his only begotten Son, that
hosoever believeth in him should not perish, but have everlasting life."
John 3:16 KJV

"that if you confess with your mouth the Lord Jesus and believe in your
heart that God has raised Him from the dead, you will be saved."
Romans10:9 NKJV

What a delight to see this
beautiful butterfly in the morning!

Did you know the caterpillar is born
to crawl, but is reborn as a butterfly?

*Therefore if any man be in Christ, he is a new creature: old
things are passed away; behold, all things are become new.*
2 Corinthians 5:17 KJV

It started to rain and the wind knocked
over the sunflowers, but be of good cheer
God brought us the morning glory...

Let's turn the pages to see
the sunflower's new friends!

This is the sunflowers first new friend Blue!

Peek-a-boo!

Angel

Purplalee Pink who is charming and sleek!

How exciting it has been learning about the love of Jesus through the sunflower garden!

What are some of your favorite things in the garden?

Enjoy the additional pictures from the garden!

Made in United States
North Haven, CT
23 April 2022

18496198R00027